THE JOYCE COUNTRY

WILLIAM
YORK
TINDALL

THE JOYCE COUNTRY

SCHOCKEN BOOKS • NEW YORK

To Cecilia and Elizabeth,
who ate cucumber sandwiches
at the Shelbourne while
I was out taking pictures

First SCHOCKEN PAPERBACK edition 1972
Second Printing, 1976
Copyright © 1960 by Pennsylvania State University
Copyright © 1972 by Schocken Books Inc.
Library of Congress Catalog Card No. 72-83501
Manufactured in the United States of America

CONTENTS

PREFACE TO THE NEW EDITION (1972)

Now there are eighty-eight pictures here. In 1954, a little after the fiftieth anniversary of Bloomsday, I took seventy-eight of these. Returning to Dublin with the same old camera in 1967, I took more pictures. Of these I have selected ten. All of them, the seventy-eight and the ten, concern what Joyce, in the first sentence of *Finnegans Wake*, called "Howth Castle and Environs" or the country of H. C. E., Bloom, Molly, Stephen, and Joyce himself. It seems suitable that these pictures, since so many of them concern *Ulysses*, appear or reappear a little after the fiftieth anniversary of this great book.

The ten additional pictures of 1967 are meant to make up for what I missed or neglected in 1954 on account of darkness, rain, or absence of mind. Now I have a picture of Howth Castle, one of the centers of *Finnegans Wake*. Taking this offered no difficulty, but the picture of Mr. Deasy's schoolhouse did. Dr. Patrick Henchy, Director of the National Library, located it for me and took me to take it—as, indeed, he took me to Howth Castle and Sidney Parade. I have also included the interior of the Gardiner Street Church, last scene of "Grace," the holy water font of All Hal-

lows, the station where Mrs. Sinico meets her train, the approximate location of the Boarding House, the clock of the Ballast Office, Stephen's University College, and the Red Bank Restaurant where Blazes Boylan partakes of oysters before going to Molly Bloom. I regret not taking the King's Inns, where Little Chandler works, and the Capuchin chapel, in Church Street, where Stephen confesses his sins. And I also regret not taking the urinal on the quays near the Four Courts (from which, in *Ulysses*, Simon Dedalus emerges) and the urinal behind St. Patrick's Cathedral (included in the *Wake* as "Saint Patrick's Lavatory"), both very dear to Joyce and both of which I have made use of. Otherwise, this book seems to me to provide a moderate, tidy accompaniment to part of Joyce's work.

It occurred to me in London, that same year, that a book similar to this could accompany T. S. Eliot's *Waste Land*, which is also enjoying its fiftieth anniversary, and his other poems. This thought came to mind when, walking on Upper Thames Street near London Bridge, I saw "Bleistein Furs" on the dusty, cracked window of a warehouse. What an illustration, I thought, to "Burbank with a Baedeker." But I was mistaken. This sign, seen on a lunch-hour excursion from Lloyd's Bank, no doubt, may have been the occasion of the poem or one of its occasions; but certainly a photograph of it could not serve as an illustration to the poem in the way a photograph of the clock of the Ballast Office can serve as an illustration to *Stephen Hero*. Photographs of Eliot's London—of St. Magnus Martyr, King William Street, and the Billingsgate Market—would do little service to *The Waste Land*. You can say that Eliot was a poet, Joyce a novelist or, in the *Wake*, a shaping wit; but that is not enough to explain the difference. Unlike Eliot, Joyce was rooted in place, and pictures of place are a proper, though partial, accompaniment.

When I went to Dublin for the first time in 1932 to see where the action in *Ulysses* took place, trams and jaunting cars were still around. When I returned to Dublin in 1954, much, I found had changed. Buses had replaced trams and motorcars had replaced jaunting cars; but many of Joyce's ingenious, lovely things were still around to tempt my camera. When I returned to Dublin in 1967, only a few vestiges of Joyce were left. They had blown Nelson's Pillar up, the pillar that is the center of Stephen's parable in *Ulysses:* "Glory be to God. They had no idea it was that high." They had torn Bloom's house down. (Why of all the houses in the row they chose Bloom's house for destruction is beyond me. I attribute it to Joyce's bad luck in Ireland or else to a conspiracy.) Only Bloom's front door was saved from the wreck. It now provides a decoration for the Bailey or Burton restaurant that once disgusted Bloom. They had torn down his mosquelike bathhouse and were starting to tear down the houses on Usher's Island, the scene of "The Dead." Mountjoy Square, where Father Conmee walked, was half gone. They had torn down most of Hardwicke Street, scene of "The Boarding House." They had carted poor Sir Philip Crampton's bust away—to a junk yard maybe. Stephen's tower had been transformed into a damp museum to be closed later on because of the damp. Elvery's Elephant House and Browne and Nolan's had moved. There were rumors that the Pigeon House was to be torn down and that the beach at Sandymount, where Stephen walks and Bloom admires Gerty, was to be filled in to provide room for warehouses and factories. At the moment, however, Pigeon House and beach are more or less intact. Someday they will blow up the Wellington Monument, if they can, as they blew up King Billy's statue that fascinated Mr. Morkan's horse, Johnny. But the cemetery is still there, and all the churches, and so, of course, the other things that in 1967 I managed to photograph. Even of these ten things of 1967 one is gone. The Red Bank Restaurant, that filled Blazes Boylan with oysters once, is restaurant no more. They converted it to a chapel. As for the seventy-eight photographs of 1954: some of them are the only memorials there are of what was once the Joyce Country. I know of no other picture of Bloom's mosque of the bath or of Sir Philip Crampton's bust, and there are few pictures, I am sure, of Bloom's house. But the pillar of "the one-handled adulterer" has been recorded many times, on postcards mostly, to be sent from Dublin with love. Nelson's Pillar was, as Joyce puts it, the heart of the Hibernian metropolis, as it remains, in a way, the heart of *Ulysses*—or, at least, a lung.

New York
Bloomsday 1972

W. Y. T.

These seventy-eight photographs of James Joyce's Dublin and its vicinity illustrate his works. Of these pictures, the first six are scenes from *Dubliners;* the eleven that follow are scenes from *A Portrait of the Artist* and *Stephen Hero;* and the rest are scenes from *Ulysses* and *Finnegans Wake.* Since Joyce's works are connected with one another, however, and since Dublin is the place of all, a good many of these pictures do double duty. Some are trivial. The Magazine in Phoenix Park, one of the centers of *Finnegans Wake,* is also the place where James Duffy of *Dubliners* sees himself at last. The Pigeon House, important in *Dubliners,* reappears in *Ulysses.* One lucky shot of Dame Street is trivial in both senses of the word: a view of the commonplace at its most commonplace, it combines significant elements of *Dubliners, Ulysses,* and *Finnegans Wake.* ("My work," said Joyce, "is less trivial than quadrivial.")

However trivial, pictures of such parts are partial in at least two senses of the word; for though a camera's eye may see the sights, they are but part of the vision. Joyce improved these sights by insight. The pictures here are of Dublin's offerings to his imagination; and since our eye is directed by his, we see more in these pictures than camera saw. Joyce's Dublin is in his books and in our minds.

When Stephen Dedalus finds Ireland important because it belongs to him (*Ulysses,* p. 629), Mr. Bloom is puzzled. We should not be puzzled had Joyce found Dublin important because it belongs to him. Dublin is important now, for us, because, belonging to Joyce, it is what he made of it. He guides our sentimental journeys to his city. No substitute for an actual visit, these pictures may help those who have not gone visiting or cannot go. Pictures in one hand, *Ulysses* or one of the other works in the other, we may approach a vision established in place. A map is also useful.

The Gracehoper was "hoppy on akkant of his joyicity" (*Finnegans Wake,* p. 414). Joyous, but not altogether joyous, Kantian Joyce—no more phenomenal than noumenal — looked at "joyicity" with mixed feelings. His obsession, it delighted and dismayed him. The center of "paralysis" and living death, his city was also the home of the Phoenix; and by the stunted houses of the quays his dirty, sacred river ran—still runs for us. Fumbally Lane may be a dismal slum, smellier than most, and Grafton Street an elegant thoroughfare, but Joyce's love and bitterness embraced them both with equal intensity. No part of Dublin—no Dubliner—was alien to him. The Joyce Country may be a district of Connemara, from which all Joyces come; but for us Dublin is that country now.

Devoted to externals, Joyce walked the streets of Dublin, noting shop, pub, church, and brothel, and every plasterer's bucket. "So This Is Dyoublong?" (*Finnegans Wake*, p. 13.) He prided himself in exile on his ability to list the shops of Talbot Street in order, down one side to Mabbot and back along the other. His devotion to such details, whether ugly or beautiful, seems all but naturalistic. So Zola must have walked the streets of Paris, notebook in hand, noting stinks and solider objects. References to Coupeau of *L'Assommoir* and to *Au Bonheur des Dames* (*Critical Writings*, pp. 43, 139) prove Joyce familiar with this earlier explorer of the modern city and master of its externals. The camera's eye might seem adequate to such vision.

Yet, however devoted to externals, the eyes of Zola and Joyce saw—as ours now see—more than eye of camera can. These pictures of Dublin, recording externals, are faithful to half of Joyce's vision. Shaun of *Finnegans Wake* is a kind of cameraman. Devoted to externals, he is centered in the eye; but his brother, Shem, devoted to the ear, is centered in the imagination. Neither the one nor the other, Joyce is the creative union of Shaun and Shem, of eye and ear, fact and imagination. Shaped by ear and imagination, what Joyce saw became the word. Sight became syllable.

However fascinating in themselves, externals of the street serve Joyce's people as occasion or stimulus for subjective vagary. In his walk down Grafton Street, pausing before Brown Thomas' shop, Bloom finds more than what is there according to the camera. What is there is there, as the picture assures us, but what he thinks and feels changes the shop entirely. For Joyce the commonplace invited greater transformation. Transfigured by a priest of the imagination, the common bread and wine of experience become radiant body. Grafton Street, though remaining Grafton Street, becomes something else and something more. What D. H. Lawrence called "the spirit of place," what G. M. Hopkins called "inscape," and what Stephen Dedalus calls "radiance" are what Joyce found, extracted, and re-embodied. As particulars of Mexico or of the English Midlands to Lawrence or as particular bird, sloe, or wreck to Hopkins, so the particulars of Dublin to Joyce. From each thing almost everything. From Dublin's landscape its inscape and the inscape or radiance of everywhere.

For Wallace Stevens, as for Joyce, there were two kinds of things: things exactly as they are and things upon the blue guitar. This blue instrument is art, of course. Things as they are are green. That Ireland is green and *Ulysses* blue—or so its original covers—improves the analogy. The wearing of the green, for Joyce, was blue.

But Baudelaire, a city man, is closer to Joyce than Stevens—closer than Zola. In "Tableaux Parisiens" Baudelaire contemplated ragpickers and rags, sewers, houses, and all the cigar butts that were to fascinate T. S. Eliot. "Elles sont grosses de suggestions," says Baudelaire. ("Was Parish worth thette mess?" asks Joyce in *Finnegans Wake*, p. 199.) Lauding the creative imagination, the great Parisian wrote essays that could be taken as commentaries on Joyce's practice—and mine. A photograph, says Baudelaire, is art's opposite; for art is never "the exact reproduction of nature." Nature—even the "paysage" of Paris—is a hieroglyph that the artist must decipher. Translated by his supernatural state of mind, ordinary things become "symbols." Bloom's Milly may assist the photographic trade at Mullingar; but Joyce's Milly is a symbol of reproduction, as her Mullingar, swarming with cows, of all fertility.

Stephen of *Stephen Hero* is another helpful commentator; for that boy could find epiphany in a grain of sand. Equivalent to his radiance, his epiphany is a showing forth and a seeing into—as when visiting Magi, seeing a baby, saw something more with this baby's co-operation. The clock of the Ballast Office, Stephen tells Cranly, is "capable of epiphany" though only "an item in the catalogue of Dublin's street furniture." "What?" says Cranly, looking at that dial. He finds it "inscrutable." (*Stephen Hero*, p. 211.) Looking at these pictures of Dublin's "street furniture" without Joyce's help, we too might find them inscrutable—and tiresome, too. What are they, after all, but pictures of streets, houses, expanses of mud, and things exactly as they are?

Such things, as capable of epiphany as Cranly's clock, acquire radiance from

Joyce. The Pigeon House, pictured here, rises from its condition as ordinary power plant to significant object by the aid of name and context: two frustrated quests, Father Butler's absence, and Mulligan's "*pigeon*," or the Holy Ghost. My picture of the bridge to the Bull shows an ordinary wooden structure that Cranly would not look at twice; yet this same bridge in *A Portrait of the Artist* becomes central revelation. A commonplace, squat tower, one of many along the coast and nothing much in a photograph, becomes in *Ulysses* an embodiment of everything maternal and paternal and all the heavy past. The Vico Road leaves suburb for all history; and a pub in Chapelizod becomes world or world in little, the very microcosm.

So Dublin itself, the sum and ghost of these pictures, is microcosm of a grander sort. In its streets Joyce saw everywhere and in its people everyone. In our time there he saw all times. Not Joyce alone, of course, but many before and after him have seen the modern city as our general symbol: Dickens in *Bleak House*, Conrad in *The Secret Agent*, Mann in *Death in Venice*, Eliot in *The Waste Land*—not to mention Zola and Baudelaire again. For some the city has proved our condition hell; but not for Joyce, who found it a purgatory with a view. His city has windows—not only Mrs. Bloom's but those two windows of "The Dead." Consider my picture of that house on Mecklenburg Street, near the corner of Mabbot. Finding encouragement even here and in the discouraging row of Eccles Street, Joyce uttered a resigned yet cheerful "yes" with something of Bloom's equanimity.

So much for Joyce's Dublin; how now about Dublin's Joyce? Outlanders, mostly Frenchmen, Germans, and Americans, together with a few Italians and Englishmen, discovered and hailed him; but Dublin has come around at last. The director of the National Library, where young Joyce filled out innumerable slips and from where he took innumerable slips away for writing verses on, has a large portrait of Joyce over his desk. Visited by Americans (me, for example), he points to it with pride. His Library has a splendid collection of Joyce's books and manuscripts, almost as rich as those at Yale, Buffalo, the British Museum, Cornell, Texas, Kansas, and Southern Illinois. Joyce who liked to think of himself as a "banned writer," might be disappointed to find Dublin bookshops displaying and selling his works.

Listing eminent graduates of University College on its centennial in 1954, the *Irish Independent*, a paper for patriots, placed Joyce first, above Padraic Pearse, the leader of the Easter Rising. (This is as if Yale, making a list, were to place Thornton Wilder above Nathan Hale or as if Columbia, making another, were to place the poet Ginsberg above Alexander Hamilton.)

The priests of Dublin, too, have come around. I have spent hours with Father E. F. O'Doherty of the National University, *Ulysses* before us on the bar, searching the text for obscure local allusions and debating Bloom's course. Did Bloom, seeking that kidney, turn south on Dorset Street or north? Father O'Doherty held out for north and I, supported by Paddy Henchy of the National Library, held out for south.

Father O'Doherty is a Dubliner. I was but a tourist, one of hundreds of academic Americans who with monograph in mind, notebook in hand, follow Bloom's way scrupulously. Dublin regards such visitors with genial amusement; but maybe Dublin learned something of Joyce from them. As Paddy Henchy ambiguously observed: "Joyce is America's gift to Ireland."

However this may be, Dublin has him now and gets along with her greatest son tolerably well. Bloomsday 1954, the fiftieth anniversary of Mr. Bloom's journey and the first to be celebrated in Dublin, is a case in point. Inflamed by Myles Na gCopaleen of the *Irish Times* (also known as Flann O'Brien and Brian Nolan), about twenty Dubliners gathered at Michael Scott's house at Sandycove on the morning of "J-Day" (June 16) to make a sentimental pilgrimage. Though they assembled as near as they could get to Stephen's tower, the idea was to follow Bloom's progress through their city. Getting away at 11:30—a little late because of Mr. Scott's hospitality—in two horse-drawn cabs and several horseless carriages, they passed Stephen's "disappointed bridge" at Kingstown (now Dun Laoghaire) on the way to Sandymount. "It's like a funeral without a body," said a celebrant. "It's a wonder they didn't think of getting a body." "I don't know anything about a body," said another celebrant, "but there's plenty of spirits about." (All this from the report in the *Irish Times*, where fifty years earlier Bloom had advertised for Martha.) Stopping at the first pub, they were dismayed by a publican who had never heard of Bloom. "Who's he?" this publican asked.

But on, on. Meeting Lennox Robinson, out with his dog for an airing, they asked him for a loan of the dog for "a little tableau on Sandymount Strand." "The back of my hand to you," or words to this effect, said Lennox Robinson. That he refused their request made no difference; for the tide was in at Sandymount, lapping the stairs from Leahy's Terrace. On to Ringsend then—but was Bloom ever there that day? They debated this until a celebrant said, no matter: the journey is "symbolic . . . not bound to keep to the original route." So they stopped at another pub to debate a choice of ways: to the Bailey Restaurant next or Eccles Street? It was then that Myles Na gCopaleen, our reporter (also known as Flann O'Brien and Brian Nolan) left this cortege for Bloom to write a report for the *Times*. We may never know on the floor of what pub the journey ended.

Maybe it got nowhere, but the gesture is far from insignificant. The symbolic action of these celebrants was the overt and spectacular part of a general excitement —of what, indeed, you might call a rising. For days before June 16 and days after, and on the day itself, the *Irish Times* devoted columns to Joyce. Prescott's Dyeworks (mentioned in *Ulysses*, p. 82) published as advertisement a portrait of Joyce. In a letter to the editor a Dubliner announced that Paddy Dignam is Homer's Elpenor and proved it like an American. The editor himself thought it likely that someday a "stony effigy" of Bloom, nobler and taller than Nelson's Pillar, would rise in Dublin. A columnist, considering plans for renaming Dublin, rejected "Joyceville" as too American and "Bloomsbury" as too British. Agreeing that "the Joyce Country is all about us," everybody thought Joyce, as tourist attraction, the Dublin Horse Show's rival.

That June a group of Dubliners met to found a James Joyce Society in the hope that "the preservation of James Joyce's memory in his native city will no longer be confined to thesis-writers from American universities." It is just as well that there has been no subsequent meeting. They order these things better on West 47th Street—as anyone can tell from an account of the proceedings there in the *New Yorker* of February 14, 1959. "Far from the Liffey" is the title of this little history.

That June, a few days too late for the Bloomsday pilgrimage, I arrived in Dublin on a Guggenheim Fellowship, like any American, to see about something in a library. Soon through with that, I spent the rest of the month and the first weeks of July with a copy of *Ulysses* in one hand, a map in the other, and a camera round my neck. My object in walking the streets, so equipped, was to see where Bloom walked. With no thought of making a book of my snaps, I snapped away for the fun of it, taking two or three hundred pictures in all. The seventy-eight pictures in this book are a selection from these. My camera is a Zeiss—a "Super Ikonta B" with Tessar lens, f 2.8. (Not altogether a commercial photographer maybe, I sold a picture once to the *New York Times*.) In spite of rain and mist, Jameson and Power, under cloud and during interludes of sun—for the sky of Dublin, as Simon Dedalus observes, is "as uncertain as a child's bottom"—this camera did justice to the scene and I to this camera. Nobody stared at me but those children on Bloom's front stoop, since Dublin is used to eccentrics.

Walking these streets, I found that many things had changed since Bloom's day. Nighttown, all but gone, is now a modern slum. The hospital of Holles Street, where Mrs. Purefoy labored, looks like an American medical center now. Gabriel Conroy's Gresham Hotel, rebuilt, looks like something in Detroit. The Ship, one of Mulligan's pubs, is no more; no more the *Freeman's Journal* and its building. Stephen's little University College has expanded beyond his recognition. And "many ingenious lovely things" are also gone—littler things. I searched for Plumtree's Potted Meat in vain and vain my search for Epps' Cocoa and for a "high grade ha" by Plasto.

Many things had changed since my first visit to Dublin in 1932. The Holles Street hospital was still Bloom's then and so was Davy Byrne's. (Mr. Byrne had a copy of *Ulysses* in the back room—or so he told me.) The trams still clanged and shunted then and jaunting cars still jingled. There is only one horseless carriage in *Ulysses*, and few were around in 1932.

But much, I found, remains much the same: Bloom's house (a little more rundown maybe), Stephen's tower, the Forty Foot, the Library, the graveyard, and Nelson's Pillar. Such vestiges are the subjects of these pictures; for there seemed little point in taking the new facade of Holles Street or of the building that has replaced Myles Crawford's office.

Some things still there I missed for one cause or another. When taken to see

Howth Castle, I failed to take my camera along, and it was dusk anyway. At Clongowes Wood College, it was raining so hard—though this is not apparent in my pictures—that I decided not to hunt the "square ditch" up. Though a constant visitor to the librarian's room, where Stephen lectures on Shakespeare, I failed to record it on film. Somehow the old building of University College did not tempt my camera.

Regretting negligence, complaining about luck, I am satisfied, nevertheless, with many of the pictures I managed to take— with most of those I have included here. My recording of the tower and Eccles Street, of Bloom's lotus-eating and lunch-hour wanderings, seems all but exemplary. Single shots of other episodes—Hades, for example—leave me little to desire; and I am no less pleased with such offbeat shots as those of Fumbally Lane and Earwicker's pub.

Of the many who helped me, I am most grateful to these: Edmund Epstein, Nora Donnelly, Patrick Henchy, and J. Mitchell Morse. Getting around the reluctant grocer who owned the tower and kept all trespassers off, Mr. Epstein secured my admission to interior and top—a rare privilege in June, 1954. Miss Donnelly, one of my two favorite Irishwomen, took me to Clongowes Wood that rainy day and did me many other favors. Mr. Henchy, one of my two favorite Irishmen, not only took me to Glendalough but introduced me to Library and tower. (And the top of the morning to Father O'Doherty.) These Dubliners prove Joyce's love of Dubliners firmly based. Mr. Morse, who saw a picture book in my pictures, did something about it.

I thank the Guggenheim Foundation, of whose generosity this book is a kind of by-product. And my thanks to St. Gregory Thaumaturgus, who helped me again.

Page references are to these editions: *The Portable James Joyce* (The Viking Press) for *Dubliners* and *A Portrait of the Artist; Finnegans Wake* (The Viking Press); *Ulysses* (Random House); *Stephen Hero*, 1944 (New Directions). I thank Mr. B. W. Huebsch and The Viking Press for permission to quote from *The Portable James Joyce* and *Finnegans Wake;* and Random House for permission to quote from *Ulysses*.

Columbia University
Bloomsday 1960

W. Y. T.

THE PIGEON HOUSE

Dublin's electric light and power station, on the
southern breakwater of the harbor, is the goal of the truant
boys in "An Encounter." "What would Father Butler be doing
out at the Pigeon House?" asks Mahony. None of
Joyce's people ever gets there. This view, from
Sandymount, is Bloom's when his eyes stray from Gerty.

FROM HERE TO "ARABY"
North Richmond Street, home of Mangan's sister
and the little boy of "Araby," is a dead end:
"An uninhabited house of two storeys stood at the blind end,
detached from its neighbors. . . . The other houses of
the street . . . gazed at one another with brown imperturbable
faces." The Christian Brothers' School is to the left.

12

THE BOARDING HOUSE
In one of these houses or another of the same sort
Mrs. Mooney, in her capacity of "Madam,"
presides over poor Mr. Doran and poor Bantam Lyons,
whose stories are continued in *Ulysses*.
The rest of Hardwicke Street has been pulled down.
Mr. Bloom's St. George's Church is off to the left
at the head of Hardwicke Street.

LITTLE CHANDLER'S LIFFEY

Crossing the bridge, in "A Little Cloud,"
Little Chandler "looked down the river towards the lower quays
and pitied the poor stunted houses. They seemed to him
a band of tramps huddled together along the river-banks. . . .
He wondered whether he could write a poem to express his idea."
Though Little Chandler was not sure
what idea he wished to express, Joyce was sure of
the idea these houses embody and show forth.

On the tracks at this station of the Kingstown to Dublin line,
Mrs. Sinico meets her train.
The newspaper finds this meeting a painful case.
Mr. Duffy's reaction is even more painful.

THE GARDINER STREET CHURCH

Cunningham, Power, and M'Coy of "Grace" take fallen
Tom Kernan here to "wash the pot." Here Father Purdon
preaches to moneylenders, pawnbrokers, and grocers
since this is Dublin's most elegant church and Jesuits
"cater for the upper classes." Father Conmee (*Ulysses*, p. 216)
lives in one of the Jesuit houses that flank the church—
as Stephen would have had he joined the Order.
(*A Portrait*, p. 420.)

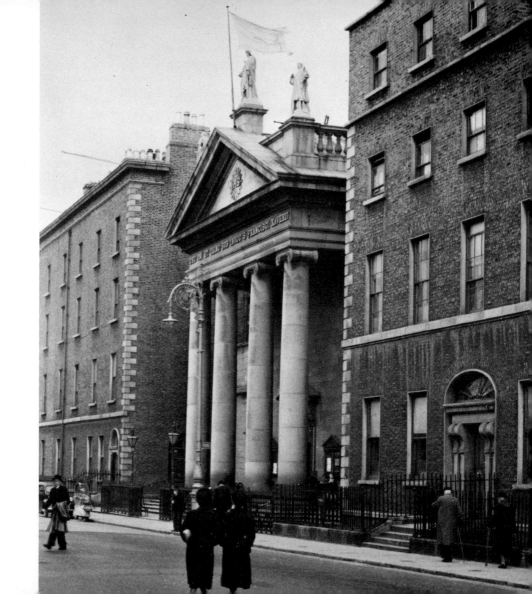

FATHER PURDON'S PULPIT

From this pulpit in the Gardiner Street Church,
Father Purdon preaches an extraordinary sermon on an
extraordinary text to the gentlemen "in the pit."
Father Purdon, says Mr. Cunningham, is
"a man of the world like ourselves."
In this church, according to Mr. Bloom,
Mrs. Bloom once sang, in soprano, an extraordinary solo,
sacred in character—as sacred, no doubt,
as Father Purdon's sermon.

The Morkan sisters occupy a "dark, gaunt house on Usher's Island," one of the quays along the Liffey. From the Morkans' windows Gabriel can see Phoenix Park and the Wellington Monument, diagonally across the river. Julia Morkan is a soprano in Adam and Eve's church, not far away to the left.

A DISTANT PROSPECT OF CLONGOWES WOOD COLLEGE
"Their fathers were magistrates, the fellows said."
Why, then, Stephen wonders, "was he sent
to that place with them?" But from the class
in elements at Clongowes at Sallins in County Kildare,
he proceeds to Ireland, Europe, the World, the Universe.
(*A Portrait*, pp. 252, 255, 267.)

CASTLE AND CHAPEL AT CLONGOWES
"There was a cold night smell in the chapel.
But it was a holy smell."
(*A Portrait*, p. 257.) Stephen's sanctuary,
however, is Father Conmee's study in the "Castle," to the left.
The classrooms and dormitories are in another building,
behind the Chapel. The playing fields are to the left and rear.

THE PLAYING FIELDS OF CLONGOWES
"The wide playgrounds were swarming with boys,"
whose "charge and thud" at football drive timid Stephen
to "the fringe of his line." (*A Portrait*, pp. 246, 248.)
The "cinderpath," where Stephen breaks his spectacles
(p. 284), is one of the first of many significant circles:
Mike Flynn's circular track (pp. 306-07); that of
the Gold Cup race in *Ulysses*; Mrs. Bloom's monologue,
turning from yes to yes; and the Vico Road
of *Finnegans Wake*. The "square ditch" is off among the trees.

"Christian brothers be damned!" says Mr. Dedalus.
"Is it with Paddy Stink and Micky Mud?
No, let him stick to the jesuits in God's name."
(*A Portrait*, p. 318.)
The archway leads to gymnasium and chapel.
It is in the main building, facing Denmark Street,
that the director, back to light,
invites Stephen to join the Order. (pp. 411-20.)

FITZGIBBON STREET

Decaying Mr. Dedalus moves his family
from suburban Blackrock to a "bare cheerless house"
on this street of "the gloomy foggy city."
(*A Portrait*, p. 312.) Discouraged, Stephen circles
"timidly round the neighboring square"
—Mountjoy Square at the top of the street.

THE BRIDGE TO THE BULL

On his way to the wading girl, Stephen meets a
squad of Christian Brothers on this "thin wooden bridge."
(*A Portrait*, pp. 424-26.) This encounter,
an epitome of *A Portrait*, reveals Stephen's pride; yet,
unlike the "disappointed bridge" of *Ulysses* (p. 26),
this bridge to the Bull seems inviting. The Bull
is a small island and the Bull Wall the northern breakwater
of Dublin harbor. Off in the distance, at the end
of the Pigeon House breakwater, is the "Poolbeg flasher."

THE WADING GIRL

Off the Bull Wall in the channels and puddles of these
mudflats, Stephen finds his image of "mortal beauty,"
her skirts pinned up. "Heavenly God!"
cries Stephen's soul. (*A Portrait*, pp. 431-32.) The place
of this encounter is more than a mile from Sandymount strand,
where Stephen takes his walk in *Ulysses*.
The hill in the distance is Howth.

ST. STEPHEN'S GREEN

The Shelbourne Hotel, visible over the trees of this urban park,
is on the northern side of what Stephen calls "my green."
Although the Shelbourne is too elegant for most of Joyce's people,
Mr. Bloom goes there to buy Mrs. Dandrade's black underthings.
(*Ulysses*, pp. 158, 524.)
Maybe Mrs. Yelverton Barry, Mrs. Bellingham,
and the Hon. Mrs. Mervyn Talboys (pp. 457-58) live here too.
Gabriel Conroy finds the Gresham more congenial.

This is the view from the Shelbourne. "Fragrant of rain,"
the trees of Stephen's Green have a "mortal odor"
in which Stephen detects the soul of his "gallant venal city."
(*A Portrait*, pp. 445-46.) Behind these gaunt houses,
which can put on majesty, Dr. Gogarty,
Stephen's Buck Mulligan, set up his practice in fashionable
Ely Place. University College is off to the right.

STEPHEN'S UNIVERSITY COLLEGE
In this building on St. Stephen's Green,
now a student center,
Stephen attends what classes he attends in
the last chapter of *A 'Portrait of the Artist*.

Stephen tells Cranly in *Stephen Hero,* as they stand just about
here, "that the clock of the Ballast Office was capable of
an epiphany" or, as he adds,
"a sudden spiritual manifestation."
In *Finnegans Wake* Joyce refers to this clock
as "clocksure off my ballast" (551)
and "ballast and ball." (518)
The Ballast Office on Westmoreland Street
is at the entrance to the O'Connell Street bridge.

46

SIR PHILIP CRAMPTON

"Is the bust of Sir Philip Crampton lyrical,
epical or dramatic?" asks Stephen. "If not, why not?"
(*A Portrait*, p. 480.) Passing Sir Philip on the way to the cemetery,
Bloom asks, "Who was he?" (*Ulysses*, pp. 91, 168.)
Isabel in *Finnegans Wake* (p. 291) is as
"inseuladed as Crampton's peartree." Peartree? More like
degenerate artichoke. Sir Philip seems Dublin's principal enigma.

THE LIBRARY PORCH
"Here," says Stephen, "I watched the birds for augury."
(*Ulysses,* pp. 214-15; *A Portrait,* pp. 491-94, 497, 501.)
Here E. C. bows to Cranly among conversing students;
and here the "darkness" of Stephen's Nashe
"falls from the air." The National Library
is on Kildare Street at the end of Molesworth Street.

MARSH'S LIBRARY
This old library, in the close of St. Patrick's Cathedral,
brings Swift to mind. Here Stephen reads
"the fading prophesies of Joachim Abbas."
(*Ulysses*, p. 40; *Stephen Hero*, p. 176.) In *Finnegans Wake* (p. 212)
"marsh narcissus" introduces a catalogue of books.

Stephen's Martello tower is about eight or nine
miles south of Dublin at Sandycove, between Kingstown
and Dalkey. This is the view from Kingstown.
The white house, not there in Stephen's day,
is the home of Michael Scott, the architect,
who bought the tower in 1954, intending a Joyce museum.

54

THE TOWER

Of the many Martello towers along the coast,
"ours is the *omphalos*," says Mulligan. (*Ulysses*, p. 19.)
Since the walls are about eight feet thick,
the barbicans give little light
to the barrel-vaulted chamber within. There is a
winding stair in the thickness of the wall. This view
is from the path to the Forty Foot, Mulligan's swimming hole.

56

Stately and plump, Buck Mulligan comes from the stairhead
with bowl of lather: *"Introibo ad altare Dei."*
Peering down "the dark winding stairs," he calls up Stephen,
his "poor dogsbody." Dog and god, dogsbody and godsbody,
are confused in Mulligan's Mass. (*Ulysses*, pp. 5, 7, 584.)
Symbolic maybe, but serving no intention,
the dog in this picture just happened to be there.
The town in the background is Kingstown.

THE PARAPET
This is the view to the south toward Dalkey
from the top of the tower. Though Stephen sees Bray Head
from here (*Ulysses*, p. 9), it is invisible.
Mulligan shaves here and Stephen thinks of mother and Fergus,
looking at the "snotgreen" sea.

As Mulligan and Haines "went down the ladder,"
Stephen "pulled to the slow iron door and locked it."
(*Ulysses*, p. 19.)
Finnegan fell from a ladder.

THE FORTY FOOT
Declaiming the ballad of joking Jesus, Mulligan
"capered before them down towards the forty foot hole."
Stephen trails his ashplant along the path. (*Ulysses*, p. 21.)
The Forty Foot is about a hundred yards from the tower.

"Give us that key," says Mulligan. (*Ulysses*, p. 24.)

In this house at Dalkey Stephen teaches a class in
Pyrrhus and Lycidas,
tutors a boy in algebra, and receives Mr. Deasy's "ducats,"
along with some good advice.
In this house Denis Florence M'Carthy,
whose poetical works are in Bloom's library,
once lived; but Bloom has read only five pages of
M'Carthy's poetical works. M'Carthy provides a connection
between Mr. Deasy (Daisy) and Mr. Flower (Bloom),
both father figures to Stephen on his way to fatherhood.

THE PLAYING FIELD OF DEASY
At the shout of "Hockey!"
the boys rush from Stephen's classroom to the grassy playing field
in front of the schoolhouse.
This field is about the size of a tennis court.
The toothless lions on the pillars of Mr. Deasy's gate
are no longer there;
but the pillars are still there.

THE STEPS FROM LEAHY'S TERRACE
Stephen's walk along the "unwholesome sandflats" starts here.
"Am I walking into eternity along Sandymount strand?"
(*Ulysses*, pp. 38-42.) Here, that evening,
Mr. Bloom looks at his Nausicaa and she at him.
Gerty's "weedgrown rocks"
(*Ulysses*, pp. 340, 347) have been replaced by a wall.

TOWARD THE PIGEON HOUSE
From the "ineluctable modality" of Sandymount strand
Stephen "turned northeast and crossed the firmer sand
towards the Pigeonhouse." Here he sees
cocklepickers, a protean dog, and a threemaster, homing;
and here, amid the flux of sand and tide,
he writes verses on a corner of Mr. Deasy's letter.
(*Ulysses*, pp. 42-51.)

No. 7, Bloom's house, is nearest the lamppost.
St. George's church is empty now and the bells no longer toll
"Heigho! Heigho!" for Paddy Dignam.

The Mater Misericordiae Hospital, to the left, is where
Dr. Dixon, now in the lying-in hospital, treated Bloom for
bee sting. "My house down there," says Bloom
as the funeral cortege passes the junction of Berkeley
and Eccles Streets, where this picture was taken. (*Ulysses*, p. 96.)

DLUGACZ'S WAY

In quest of kidney, Bloom proceeds from Eccles Street
to Dorset Street. Passing the pub on the corner,
he says, "Good day, Mr. O'Rourke."
Dlugacz's butcher shop was probably in the row
of shops on the farther side of Dorset Street.
(*Ulysses*, pp. 57-59.)

AGENDATH NETAIM
"To catch up and walk behind ... her moving hams."
Failing in this, Mr. Bloom "walked back along Dorset street,
reading gravely Agendath Netaim." (*Ulysses*, pp. 59-61.)
Bloom's house is behind O'Rourke's Sandeman sign,
under the third chimney from the right.

With Martha's letter in pocket and "high grade ha"
on head, Mr. Bloom passes "the drooping nags of the hazard."
This cab stand, next to the Westland Row station,
is on Brunswick Street, now Pearse Street. (*Ulysses*, pp. 75-76.)

THE GROSVENOR

Here at the corner of Brunswick Street and Westland Row,
Bloom meets M'Coy, discovers Plumtree's Potted Meat,
and sees (or all but sees) a lady climbing into
a jaunting car. "Watch! Watch! Silk flash rich stockings. . . .
A heavy tramcar honking its gong slewed between."
The "Loop Line bridge," next to the
Grosvenor, leads into the Westland Row station, to the left.
(*Ulysses*, pp. 72-75.)

ALL HALLOWS
This church on Westland Row,
beyond the Loop Line bridge, is actually St. Andrew's.
"*Corpus.* Body. Corpse," says Eucharistic Bloom.
"Iron nails ran in." (*Ulysses*, pp. 78-82.)
Noting the "low tide of holy water," Bloom leaves the
church and walks down Westland Row toward Lincoln Place.

As Mr. Bloom goes out of All Hallows and pauses on the porch,
his eye on this font,
he notices the level of the holy water.
This font is only one of the many vessels
in a chapter of pots and tubs.
Consider Plumtree's Potted Meat and the Gold Cup race.
After all, the symbol of the Lotus-eating chapter is
the Eucharist and that comes in chalice and ciborium.
Eucharistic Bloom sits, at last, in a tub.

Sweny the Chemist, at the junction of Westland Row
and Lincoln Place, provides Bloom with lemon soap.
(His successor does not stock this kind.)
Near Sweny's Bloom gives Bantam Lyons the tip on Throwaway.
(*Ulysses*, pp. 82-84.)

THE BATH
Rid of Bantam, Bloom walks "cheerfully towards
the mosque of the baths." "This is my body,"
says Narcissistic Jesus-Bloom,
contemplating a "languid floating flower."
(*Ulysses*, p. 85.) No longer a bath,
the "mosque" of Lincoln Place is warehouse now.
Hornblower's gate is across the street.

"POOR DIGNAM"
From Paddy Dignam's house, 9 Newbridge Avenue,
Sandymount (near Leahy's Terrace), the funeral cortege
proceeds to Glasnevin cemetery on the other side of Dublin.
Cunningham, Power, Dedalus, and Bloom enter their carriage here.
On his way to Nausicaa, Bloom returns
to Paddy's house to comfort the widow. (*Ulysses*, pp. 86, 631.)

BLAZES BOYLAN'S RED BANK
Just after passing Plasto's High Grade Hats and
Sir Philip Crampton's bust,
Paddy Dignam's funeral cortege passes the Red Bank Restaurant,
from which Blazes Boylan, jaunty in a new straw hat, emerges,
"airing his quiff."
"Worst man in Dublin," thinks Bloom.
At Davy Byrne's for lunch, Bloom thinks again of Boylan
and Red Bank oysters: "Effect on the sexual. Aphrodis.
He was in the Red Bank this morning."
And, as Bloom knows, Boylan is on his way to Molly.

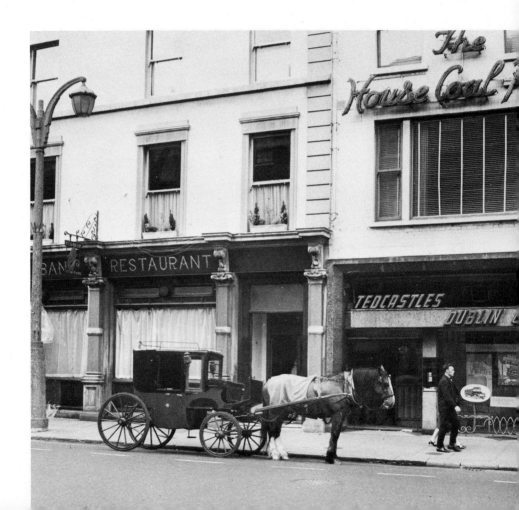

WAITING FOR PADDY
After toad-bellied Father Coffey's hasty service
at the Mortuary Chapel,
Glasnevin, the gravediggers put Paddy's coffin
on this "coffincart" or another like it. (*Ulysses*, pp. 101-03.)

ERECTED BY
PATRICK BARNES,
OF 105 JAMES'S STREET,
IN MEMORY OF
HIS BELOVED MOTHER
ANNE BARNES,
WHO DIED 2ND AUGUST 1895,
AGED 81 YEARS
HERE ALSO ARE INTERRED
THE REMAINS OF THE ABOVE NAMED
PATRICK BARNES,
WHO DIED 1st MAY 1898,
AGED 46 YEARS
ALSO VIOLET, DEARLY LOVED WIFE OF
JOHN T. O'REILLY,
WHO DIED 20TH DECEMBER 1922.
R. I. P.

AND THE ABOVE
JOHN T. O'REILLY
ST RAPHAEL, STILLORGAN ROAD,
WHO DIED 7TH MAY 1934

THE ONEHANDLED ADULTERER
At the foot of Nelson's Pillar (O'Connell Street)
the two vestals buy four and twenty plums,
then "waddle slowly up the winding staircase. . . .
Glory be to God. They had no idea it was that high."
(*Ulysses*, pp. 143, 146.) The Post Office
is to the left and the Gresham Hotel in the background.

Those two wise virgins "have lived fifty and fifty-three
years in Fumbally's lane." "Where is that?"
asks Professor MacHugh. Here it is.
Those old girls set out from here for Nelson's Pillar,
plums, and a Pisgah sight of dear, dirty Dublin.
(*Ulysses*, p. 143.) Fumbally Lane
is not far from St. Patrick's Cathedral and The Coombe.

THE HEART OF THE HIBERNIAN METROPOLIS
Telling his Parable of the Plums
to Miles Crawford, J. J. O'Molloy, and Professor MacHugh,
Stephen pauses here, before the statue of Sir John Gray,
amid shunting trams. (Trams no more—busses now.)
O'Molloy glances wearily at Nelson's hand.
"Tickled the old ones too," says Crawford.
(*Ulysses*, pp. 115, 147-48.)

"My casting vote is: Mooney's," says Lenehan.
After the parable, he leads the pressgang across
O'Connell Street toward this pub,
where treating Stephen spends Deasy's ducats.
(*Ulysses*, pp. 142, 146.) Mooney's *en ville*
is on Abbey Street, not far from the theater.

"A sombre Y.M.C.A. young man, watchful among the warm fumes
of Graham Lemon's, placed a throwaway in a hand of Mr. Bloom."
Lemon's sweet shop is on
O'Connell Street near Elvery's Elephant House, where the man
in the macintosh buys macintoshes,
no doubt, and Gabriel "goloshes." (*Ulysses*, p. 149.)

FEEDING THE GULLS

On the O'Connell Bridge Bloom throws Elijah's throwaway
away and sees K. 11 in the river.
"Mr. Bloom smiled O rocks at two windows of the ballast office."
(*Ulysses*, pp. 150-52.) The Ballast Office
is the building to the right on the corner of Westmoreland Street.
The "timeball" is no longer there
but the clock still is—on the Westmoreland Street side.
According to Stephen (*Stephen Hero*, p. 211)
even this commonplace clock is "capable of an epiphany."

Here Bloom meets Mrs. Breen, H. E. L. Y. 'S, and Farrell,
who walks outside the lampposts.
Passing the office of the *Irish Times*,
Bloom remembers his advertisement for Martha.
(*Ulysses.* pp. 152-58.)

DAME STREET

Mr. Bloom once worked for Hely's; and Hely himself was one of Mrs. Bloom's suitors. Hely is a stationer.

"I was going along Dame Street," says Corley of "Two Gallants," "and I spotted a fine tart under Waterhouse's clock."

This clock, with letters on the dial instead of figures, appears throughout *Finnegans Wake*. (E.g., pp. 88, 213.)

Serving as Eucharist, Earwicker's "baken head" becomes a loaf of "Singpantry's Kennedy bread." (p. 7.)

THE MEETING OF THE WATERS
Near Trinity College and the Bank, Bloom
"crossed under Tommy Moore's roguish finger. They did right
to put him up over a urinal: meeting of the waters."
(*Ulysses*, p. 160.) "The meeting of the waters"
(from Moore's verses on the Vale of Avoca)
becomes a motif in *Finnegans Wake*. (E.g., p. 96.)

Walking past "Trinity's surly front" (*Ulysses*, p. 162),
Bloom meets Parnell's brother: "Poached eyes on ghost."
College Green at the foot of Dame Street
(our present point of view) is site of the statue of King Billy
that fascinated old Morkan's horse.
The unfascinated Irish tore this statue down—as they would tear
Nelson's Pillar down but for the cost of the tearing.

Bloom "crossed at Nassau street corner
and stood before the window of Yeates and Son."
It is here that, eclipsing the sun with his little finger,
he meditates on parallax. Grafton Street lies before us.
Browne and Nolan's is off to the left on Nassau Street.

(*Ulysses,* p. 164.)

"Gay with . . . awnings," Dublin's Fifth Avenue
"lured his senses." Brown Thomas' shop
and Combridge's corner are to the left. (*Ulysses*, pp. 165, 166.)

DUKE STREET
The "Burton" (actually the Bailey), where Bloom
has his vision of Lestrygonians slopping food up,
is to the left. Davy Byrne's sign is to the right.
The Bailey is now one of Dublin's better restaurants.

Nosey Flynn is there, dripping, when Bloom enters
for Burgundy and "feety" Gorgonzola.
As the Burton has changed for the better,
so Davy Byrne's for the worse. All red leather
and chromium now, it caters to another sort entirely.
The exterior remains the same.
At Duke Lane, a dog chokes up "a sick knuckly cud"
as Bloom passes on his way to Dawson Street.
(*Ulysses*, pp. 169-77.)

MOLESWORTH STREET
Having helped the blind stripling across
Dawson Street (in the background) and into Molesworth Street,
masonic Bloom passes Freemasons' Hall.
(*Ulysses*, pp. 178-80.)

Molesworth Street leads to Kildare Street
where Library and Museum stand side by side.
"To the right. Museum. Goddesses. . . . Cold statues: quiet there.
Safe in a minute. . . . Ah, soap there! Yes. Gate. Safe!"
(*Ulysses*, pp. 180-81.)
There no more, those goddesses have yielded to Irish crosses.

SCYLLA AND CHARYBDIS

Through this gate, Bloom emerges with "step of a pard," having passed safely between Mulligan and Stephen at the door. (*Ulysses*, pp. 214-15.)

LIBRARY

An Ċneó Irceac
An Leabarlann Náiriúnca aġur
Árd-Scoil Náiriúnca na hEalaḋan

Entrance
to The National Library and
The National College of Art

MOUNTJOY SQUARE
From the Jesuit house in Gardiner Street,
Father Conmee proceeds to Mountjoy Square where he meets
and blesses a onelegged sailor.
This decorous square is not unlike decorous Father Conmee.
(*Ulysses*, pp. 216-17.)

Dillon's auction room ("Barang!") is across
the river on Bachelors' Walk.
Ben Dollard crosses the quay "from the metal bridge . . .
scratching actively behind his coattails."
Simon Dedalus says: "Hold that fellow with the bad trousers."
(*Ulysses*, pp. 230, 233, 240-41.)

THE SWEETS OF SIN
"A darkbacked figure under Merchant's arch
scanned books on the hawker's car": "*costliest frillies.
For him!* . . . *her heaving embonpoint.*" (*Ulysses*, pp. 224, 232-33.)
Merchant's Arch is bare of books today,
but the archway still leads hopefully to the Liffey.

The Ormond Hotel is the haunt of Bloom's Sirens.
(*Ulysses*, pp. 252, 253.) The interior, reconstructed,
no longer resembles the place of Bloom's dinner and
Simon's song. The exterior is much the same, no doubt,
as when Miss Kennedy and Miss Douce
"heard the viceregal hoofs go by, ringing steel."

144

BARNEY KIERNAN'S

This pub (8, 9, and 10 Little Britain Street) is the cave
of Bloom's Cyclops; but pub no more,
Barney's premises are warehouses now. It is around
this corner that Bloom, in Cunningham's jaunting car,
ascends "to the glory of the brightness at an angle
of forty-five degrees over Donohoe's in Little Green Street
like a shot off a shovel." (*Ulysses*, pp. 334, 339.)

There are no jaunting cars in Dublin now,
no "outsiders" that is. But this car, though a kind of insider,
is of a family with jaunty jingling Boylan's
and Martin Cunningham's. Cork has jaunting cars aplenty.
(*Ulysses*, pp. 272, 335.)

STAR OF THE SEA

Parish church of Paddy Dignam and Gerty MacDowell,
the Star of the Sea is at the corner of Leahy's Terrace
and the Tritonville Road.
Celebrating Mary, this church presides over Gerty on the shore.
From its altar "the perfume of those incense,"
from its belfry those bats,
and in its rectory Bloom's cuckoo clock.
Sandymount strand is directly behind the church.
(*Ulysses*, pp. 340-75.)

When Bloom worked with cows, he lived at this hotel,
54 Prussia Street, next to the Cattle Market.
"I was up at that meeting in the City Arms. . . .
Cattle traders, says Joe, about the foot and mouth disease."
(*Ulysses*, pp. 288, 664-65.)

FOOT AND MOUTH

Dignam's funeral cortege meets a drove of fertile cattle, "blocking up the thoroughfare." Bullockbefriending Bloom dreams of "a tramline along the North Circular from the cattle market to the quays." Bullockbefriending Stephen takes Mr. Deasy's letter to the press. Milly is "beef to the heels" in cattle-crowded Mullingar. "Horned and capricorned," the "zodiacal host" of this picture is bursting from the Cattle Market, where Bloom once worked. "Parallax stalks behind and goads" these Oxen of the Sun. (*Ulysses*, pp. 58, 96, 97, 407, 664.) Stephen's moocow is quiet, but the bulls of Finnegan bellow, "Boyarka buah!" The bull of the Mookse is papal. (*Finnegans Wake*, pp. 152, 198.)

This house on Mecklenburg Street, near Mabbot,
is one of the few surviving houses of Nighttown.
Bella Cohen's place may have been something like this one,
which seems entirely suitable
for the metaphysics of Mecklenburg Street.

GUMLEY
On their way from Circe to Eumaeus, Bloom and Stephen
pause here to observe Gumley, guarding cobblestones.
Corley asks for a handout.
The Loop Line railroad carried Stephen and Bloom from
Westland Row to the Amiens Street station, near Nighttown,
as it once carried the little boy from Amiens Street to "Araby."

The cabman's shelter of Skin-the-Goat is
"an unpretentious wooden structure" at Butt Bridge.
The railway bridge,
next to Butt Bridge, carries the Loop Line over the Liffey.
(*Ulysses*, pp. 603, 605.)

ITHACA

At a ground-floor window of 7 Eccles Street a
"bare generous arm" and "taut shiftstraps"
shine briefly as Molly throws a coin
"over the area railings" to a onelegged sailor.
Climbing over these railings, keyless Bloom drops into the area,
thirty-two feet per second. His parlor with its stuffed owl
occupies the ground floor front. His kitchen,
where cocoa is produced, looks upon the area from the basement.
Molly's bedroom is on the ground floor to the rear.
(*Ulysses*, pp. 222, 652-53.)

The Liffey, which bisects the town, is invisible
from here, but Earwicker's pub is conspicuous and central.
Phoenix Park occupies the background.
The Wellington Monument is on the horizon to the right.
Scene of Tristan's visit to Isolde
and of Earwicker's fall and rise, Chapelizod
is also the home of James Duffy, a painful case.

Earwicker's pub on the Mullingar Road still serves Jameson and Guinness. The present publican has never heard of Joyce, however, still less of Earwicker. Generally called the Mullingar (*Finnegans Wake*, pp. 64, 138, 286, 321, 345, 370, 371, 380), Earwicker's pub is sometimes called the Bristol (pp. 133, 392, 405, 539, 606, 624).

Bristol, derived from "bridge," may imply the bridge across the Liffey, directly in front of the pub, or the Bridge Inn, across the river. As dual as Earwicker, his pub may occupy both banks, Shem's and Shaun's.

Earwicker is the hill as Anna the river.
The head of the sleeping giant lies here. Howth Castle
is at the base of the peninsula, far away to the right.
Beyond the Bailey lighthouse and across Dublin Bay
is Stephen's tower. Bray Head is in the remote background.
Where are Bloom's rhododendrons?
Molly's "O rocks" may refer to Gibraltar and Howth.
"I'm tired of all them rocks in the sea,"
says the ancient mariner. (*Ulysses*, p. 614.)

The "riverrun" of the first sentence of the *Wake* proceeds
from Adam and Eve's Church to "Howth Castle and Environs"
or H. C. E. The famous hill of rhododendrons,
where Bloom received a bit of seedcake from Molly,
is off to the left.
Jarl van Hoother of Howth Castle,
in the first chapter of the *Wake*,
is plagued by the Prankquean. "Am liking it," she says.

170

THE WELLINGTON MONUMENT

Somewhere around here in Phoenix Park Earwicker meets the Cad. Pointing to the "*duc de Fer's* overgrown milestone," Earwicker says: "I am woowoo willing to take my stand . . . upon the monument, that sign of our ruru redemption." In Hosty's ballad Earwicker was "joulting by Wellington's monument. . . . When some bugger let down the backtrap of the omnibus." Wellington's monolith (or "monomyth") becomes the "mormorial" of Earwicker's Waterloo. (*Finnegans Wake*, pp. 8, 36, 47, 335, 543, 581.) In "The Dead," the snow forms "a bright cap on the top of the Wellington Monument."

THE MAGAZINE

As giant, H. C. E. lies dormant "from the macroborg of Holdhard [Howth] to the microbirg of Pied de Poudre [the Magazine]. Behove this sound of Irish sense." Although the lesser of Earwicker's "two mounds," Swift's Magazine in Phoenix Park is the scene of Earwicker's fall; for two girls and three soldiers lurk in the "follyages" around here. Joining the Wellington Monument, the Magazine becomes museum, midden, and dump or *Finnegans Wake* itself. On this hill James Duffy of "A Painful Case" finds himself alone. (*Finnegans Wake*, pp. 7-8, 12-13.)

On the banks of the Liffey at Chapelizod
two washerwomen make Earwicker's "private linen public."
Where are elm and stone? But it is plain that Liffey is "leafy":
"I am leafy speaking," says A. L. P., who is also little
"Anna Rayiny, when unda her brella,
mid piddle med puddle she ninnygoes nannygoes nancing by."
This portrait of Anna is from the bridge at Chapelizod.
The Mullingar is off to the right.
(*Finnegans Wake*, 7, 196-216, 619.)

ADAM AND EVE'S

Finnegans Wake begins with "riverrun past Eve and Adam's. . . ."
Adam and Eve's is the parish church of the Morkans.
The courthouse in the background (place of Earwicker's trial?)
is on the other bank of the Liffey.

Having passed the church, "riverrun" becomes
"a commodius vicus of recirculation"; for
"The Vico road goes round and round to meet where terms begin."
(*Finnegans Wake*, pp. 3, 452.) We have come
a long way from the cinderpath of *A Portrait*. The Vico Road
runs south from Dalkey around Killiney Bay towards Bray.

The legend of St. Kevin of Glendalough
(*Finnegans Wake*, pp. 604-06) celebrates Kevin-Shaun
or Earwicker again. Out of this graveyard renewal.
Glendalough of the seven churches
is in County Wicklow to the south of Dublin.

Lizzie A. Graham
Joseph Keenan
who died Mar. 11th 1929
also his wife
Brigid Keenan